Praise for *The Boo*

"Congratulations to Rob Carney ᴏ.. .ᴜs winning manuscript, *The Book of Drought.* One of the most original and powerful manuscripts I've come across in years!"

—**RICHARD BLANCO**

"During drought, everything becomes dust. Rob Carney's newest book elegizes this loss, offers poignant odes to dry streambeds and withered plants, tells fables about vanished bears, herons, and lighting. The poetics are deft. Carney's work has long amazed with his sometimes rowdy, always memorable music. This book, though, is written with restraint. The poems often feel like we're eavesdropping on conversations—sad anecdotes of barely remembered rivers, sharp longings for vanished blossoms. But these voices aren't always wistful: the young inheritors of this desolation lament and rage. Who can blame them? They may never sink their feet in mud, jump carefree into icy water. And yet, by the end of this book, we also hear a whisper of hope. The last section—'If the drought breaks'—speaks of the possibility of mud and snails, the return of trees. *The Book of Drought* speaks to our moment. It is the best book of poetry that I've read in years."

—**TOD MARSHALL,** Washington State Poet Laureate

"*The Book of Drought* weaves a song of loss and irrevocably changed landscapes. With an empathy for those dispossessed of such places, Carney's couplets invoke both 'the sorrow of glaciers' and the power of poetry to pass on that loss. Water, and its lack, is the tenor of the song, binding people together with poignancy, humor, and, in the end, hope. Essential reading."

—**DANIEL SPOTH,** author of *Ruin and Resilience* and Board Member of the Association for the Study of Literature and the Environment

THE BOOK OF DROUGHT

THE BOOK
OF DROUGHT

Poems

Rob Carney

Winner of The 2023 X. J. Kennedy Poetry Prize
Selected by Richard Blanco

TRP: The University Press of SHSU
Huntsville, Texas 77341

Library of Congress Cataloging-in-Publication Data
Names: Carney, Rob, 1968- author.
Title: The book of drought : poems / Rob Carney.
Description: First edition. | Huntsville : TRP: The University Press of
    SHSU, [2024] | "Winner of The 2023 X. J. Kennedy Poetry Prize, selected
    by Richard Blanco."
Identifiers: LCCN 2024009347 (print) | LCCN 2024009348 (ebook) | ISBN
    9781680033922 (paperback) | ISBN 9781680033939 (ebook)
Subjects: LCSH: Droughts—Poetry. | Dystopias—Poetry. | LCGFT: Poetry. |
    Science fiction poetry. | Ecopoetry.
Classification: LCC PS3603.A7653 B66 2024 (print) | LCC PS3603.A7653
    (ebook) | DDC 811/.6—dc23/eng/20240229
LC record available at https://lccn.loc.gov/2024009347
LC ebook record available at https://lccn.loc.gov/2024009348

FIRST EDITION

Cover image: *Not a Drop to Drink*, by Elena Soterakis
Author photo by Jennifer Woznick

Cover design by Cody Gates, Happenstance Type-O-Rama
Interior design by Maureen Forys, Happenstance Type-O-Rama

Printed and bound in the United States of America
First Edition Copyright: 2024

TRP: The University Press of SHSU
Huntsville, Texas 77341
texasreviewpress.org

Winner of The 2023 X. J. Kennedy Poetry Prize
Selected by Richard Blanco

Established in 1998, The X. J. Kennedy Prize highlights one full-length collection of poetry per year.

PREVIOUS WINNERS:

Sebastian Merrill, *GHOST :: SEEDS*

Kathleen Rooney, *Where Are the Snows*

Brooke Sahni, *Before I Had the Word*

Caroline M. Mar, *Special Education*

Garret Keizer, *The World Pushes Back*

Jay Udall, *Because a Fire in Our Heads*

Jeff Hardin, *No Other Kind of World*

Gwen Hart, *The Empress of Kisses*

Corinna McClanahan Schroeder, *Inked*

Ashley Mace Havird, *The Garden of the Fugitives*

Jeff Worley, *A Little Luck*

James McKean, *We Are the Bus*

George Drew, *The View from Jackass Hill*

Joshua Coben, *Maker of Shadows*

Ashley Renee, *Basic Heart*

William Baer, *"Bocage" and Other Sonnets*

Becky Gould Gibson, *Aphrodite's Daughter*

Deborah Bogen, *Landscape with Silos*

Lee Rudolph, *A Woman and a Man, Ice-Fishing*

Eric Nelson, *Terrestrials*

Jan Lee Ande, *Reliquary*

Jorn Ake, *Asleep in the Lightning Fields*

Barbara Lau, *The Long Surprise*

Philip Heldrich, *Good Friday*

Gray Jacobik, *The Surface of Last Scattering*

For my wife

Contents

IV. Lessons

V. Bonds

VI. Fables

VII. Bones

VIII. Rain

I
Origins

WE PAINT THE ROCKS BLUE

so they look less like tombstones.
So the riverbeds—dry now,

just paths for deer to walk—
seem less like ghosts.

In our pockets: all the insults we carry,
insults we place on the flat slab under the falls,

or what used to be the falls when snow still fell
and March became a watersong of melting.

For instance, keys
to whatever dispossessions.

Or the envelopes declaring, "Final Notice,"
those red words

fading in the sun now,
held in place with stones.

A lapel pin—meaningless—
"To commemorate 25 years of service."

And a necklace improvised from fishing line,
sim cards, and rings...

≈

we leave our relics here,
and coins the crows might find a reason for,

and maybe the weight
feels lighter now,

maybe there's room
for the wind to fit somewhere.

It used to usher clouds overhead,
and sometimes a few of them would open.

First, birds arriving and lining up on branches.
Then the rain.

≈

Now all that swims here are memories.
Not fish in the pools

below waterfalls. Not fish
rising—*plip*—to the surface,

and dragonflies *gone*.
Those fish are as gone as the water.

Not the wind, although, yes,
there are gusts sometimes,

but the leaves to swim through
are missing.

And no constant murmur over stones;
the rivers are gone. There's nothing but us now.

≈

This river looked like a diamondback—
its sandbars raised, and black boulders—

snaking its way through the heat
baked daily into cliffs.

And this one followed the elk's migration.
And this one used to have a name.

And this one, wider, made you shield your eyes—
that bright,

its shimmer
electric on the surface.

And this dry river was the site of a wedding
between an aspen forest and the moon.

The sky gave the Future as a gift,
but it didn't say what kind.

≈

I guess you could call us all *amateur* pilgrims.
Not ready to formalize rituals.

Not ready to believe forever
that the rains are gone,

that *rain* is just a meaningless word,
a lapel pin "For 25 centuries of service."

Instead, we follow the forecasts
and hope they're true.

There's a current, for instance, in the Sea of Cortez,
stirring storms in a northerly direction.

And a rumor out of Arizona that they've seen clouds,
that a few seem promising.

≈

On our Wall of Rhetorical Questions,
we like to carve jokes.

Carve, *Why is this happening?*
Carve, *What do you think of this weather we're having?*

And, *When will it*
get back to normal?

And, *Who could've known?*
They're our bland hieroglyphics:

no feathered gods,
no Staff-With-Gleaming-Headpiece,

just re-arrangements of the alphabet, but we smile,
and the kids need to see that sometimes.

≈

This one moves like a butterfly,
fluttering her costume.

And this one
listens like jaybird—tilted head.

That one carries his quiet around. It's a shell
to duck in when his parents start fighting.

And this one sleeps the way a cat sleeps:
chin tucked in.

There are always some kids here too,
dragged along like it's Sunday.

But an empty river isn't church.
And you can throw rocks as far as you want to.

≈

I've forgotten, now, why I'm telling you this.
The doctors say, "It's one of the symptoms."

I say doctors are hilarious
but probably mean well.

I remember one time
there were blackberries growing—

not greenhouse vines,
just wherever.

You could stand there and eat them if you wanted:
small gifts from the rain.

•

II
Gathering

BACK WHEN WATER WAS AN ELEMENT,

hydrologists would measure things:
the depth of the rivers,

aridity of soil cores,
the sorrow of glaciers

as they faded,
disappeared.

They had inches, and acre feet,
and flashes of level-headed anger—

Remember when you used to go cliff-jumping?
My advice is don't—

I'm saying, they had numbers,
stacked data.

All I've got are buckets down a well,
just some language at the bottom if I'm lucky.

Like maybe I can pull up
another word for *zero*.

Then some other words, too, a whole sentence,
that sounds a bit like hope.

≈

They held a vote.
I'm the one they elected

to be the Listener and Reservoir and Scribe—
the one who records this.

Say, the green of a hummingbird's feathers
as it hovers,

then the shapeshift purple
when it moves.

Say, the sound of a lake
against a boat dock: like tucking in a child,

or like *slosh*
whenever wakes come rolling.

"Write it all," they tell me,
so I fill up the margins.

I can't be yet another thing
that lets them down,

≈

but the past tense is everywhere.
How long, for instance,

since a hummingbird's been spotted?
How long

since we couldn't just walk across a lake,
the bed of it cracked now, bed of it dust,

dance partner of the wind
if the wind were a cough?

Nobody knows since we don't count back;
all the seasons mean subtraction already:

no snow in the winter months,
feathering through lamplight;

no rain in the spring months
and cold drops running down your shirt.

≈

"It began with a shiver," she says,
"like I knew this tulip

was the last one I'd see in my yard.
Not the cold outside—

I had a jacket on—
but that shiver, you know, when you're surprised?

I kept looking at that flower, that red,
so I wouldn't forget."

≈

He tells me: "The wind
is what gets us,

especially at night
with so many trees dead now.

We think we hear the baby crying,
but the baby's fine.

There's just no leaves anymore,
no leaves for that sway-sound and rustle.

When the wind cuts through,
it makes a pitch the same as crying."

≈

Don't ask me yet
about the animals.

You're right,
but don't ask about the animals.

≈

The world was the world, and beautiful
but lonely. Valleys

divided the mountains,
each from each.

The sky had the sun and the moon,
and light connecting them.

The ocean had tides joining *in* and *out*
like song, two voices in harmony.

No, only the mountains had to go through life apart,
so the world sent clouds to be an answer.

The clouds brought snow—
a shared blanket through the winter.

And the snow piled deep—
a shared dream.

And in the spring,
as the days warmed,

the mountains woke to find rivers.
And those rivers braided the mountains into *one*.

≈

Back when water was an element,
that story didn't need telling.

Now, when I do,
I see sadness in some,

or disbelief.
A few of them talk to me—

words,
like they're filling up a river,

words I've been picked to remember
and pass on to you.

•

III
Reconstructing
Fragments

RULES FOR THE NAME-THAT-MEMORY CONTEST:

1. Nothing anatomical, please.

2. No kissing stories either. If you don't believe me, go and ask your kids.

3. No one wins a prize for this. The prize is the act of remembering, and of finding out that language is a span bridge—here to there, from nowhere to somewhere new after.

4. Try to act responsibly. Your memory will enter into other people's memories.

5. Drop your entry in this coffee can, unsigned.

≈

Entry 1:

My nana and papa had a peach tree, with peaches, and I wish I could eat them like we used to. Drowt.

Papa would lift me up to see if they were loose, or maybe needed five more minutes, and even up under the leaves where some would hide. He was strong 'cause I was big now, four.

And when one of the branches poked Nana in her eye, he got a saw and set me on his shoulders so I could cut it down 'cause I never ever did it before, but I can. I said, "You asshole branch," and Nana laughed, and then her eye didn't hurt.

That's how strong my papa was. This much.

≈

Entry 2:

I guess I took up paddle boarding just in time. Enough to get a few years in. It isn't too hard to balance, but enough, like you sort of feel good, like it's a challenge. And the water, when there used to be water, wasn't too deep. It was still pretty warm if you ever fell in, especially for snow, and this was all snowfall melted from the mountains.

They'd be white at the top, whether sun and blue or overcast, and stayed white until the end of June. And the only real sounds were our paddles—swooshing and swooshing but musical, kind of, and the wind. That was the other sound too. Like these short and long Sky-Breaths skuffing past your ears.

≈

Entry 3:

I understand why the cities had to do it, but it makes me sad: to

never see a pond in a park.

And no grass, of course. That's a goner like everything else.

I used to like the blue jays there, how they'd cock one eye and

squawk at me for peanuts, 'til the seagulls and squirrels took over and

drove the jays away.

Still, I'd settle for a seagull again. Something that loops on the

wind, or just drifts there.

Wings out, remember? Wild and easy.

Like a living kite.

≈

Entry 4:

Sorry, all I picture are the wildfires everywhere.

≈

Entry 5:

I used to think, Who would ever come here? It's not a concert. It

isn't theater. And it isn't a cult, not that I would join one. There are too

many wind-up zombies already. Anyway, I wondered, Why come here?

but I did, so this is my memory:

When I said we should paint the rocks blue, nobody laughed.

And they came back with brushes.

No one ever thought I had a good idea before.

≈

Entry 6:

Even if you never dropped a line in the water, so you don't really know what that's about, just trust me: The sound of it, plunk, *casting out was a kind of proof that there was meaning.*

Even before *you felt a strike. Before that voltage came spiking from the water. Up through your hand, up through your blood-jump, and all the way down to your heels, two pulses in your boots.*

Even on the days it would rain, and every drop—a million billion—drew a circle on the surface. And someone brought their dog along, with that wet-fur smell that carries everywhere.

And of course all of this was just catch-&-release, so you're never going to get that trout-taste sizzle… even then, that plunk *was worth everything.*

So where did it go?

≈

And the titles of these entries, if you're wondering, in no particular order:

> "The First Time I Thought, Really Thought, I Might Have Friends"

> "Why Blue Is My Favorite Color"

> "Helping Papa Eat Peaches"

> "Fishing"

> "As If the Whole Day Is Talking to You"

> "I know you meant well, but I don't like this game"

•

IV
Lessons

KIDS CUT RIGHT THROUGH THE NONSENSE;

when the governor comes on the news, for instance,
advising us we need to pray for rain,

a girl just groans
and walks off disgusted, saying,

"What kind of bullshit God
wouldn't already know?…

I mean, look!"—
throwing her arms wide open, a gesture

to sweep in the whole panorama—
"The forests are nothing

but a box of burnt matchsticks.
What the fuck?"

She should be our ambassador.
Or someone who learns to play guitar.

We could siphon off juice from the power plant, get her amp,
and make that the chorus.

She could call her song "The Rain Prayer"
and teach it to the rest.

≈

Not all of them are so well-spoken,
but there's time.

We're all still adjusting,
and they're still young,

still working out the punch
and shimmy of verbs.

Like this boy, first grade,
always naming what's around him:

"Hi, Rock-
That-My-Arm-Wants-to-Slingshot."

"Hi, Ram-on-the-Ridge-
Who-Is-a-Ghost."

"Hi, Thorn-in-My-Foot-
Through-the-Hole-in-My-Shoe."

"I hate thorns."

≈

His older sister—
turning eight soon, I think—

has a wind-up line
she always uses:

"My dad says you're the Recorder,
so you can write this down"…

≈

"Now, this is 'The Story of Cats'—
Once upon a time, there were two,

and they were friends,
and both of them were black-and-white

or white-and-gray,
a little like a panda face,

and they looked like a curled-up panda when they slept,
but this is not a sleeping story.

This is the story
of people being hungry...

But the cats were never hungry 'cause they could chase,
and they liked to eat grasshoppers.

How many grasshoppers were there?
Just try counting to infinity.

Mostly the land was all dead,
but the land still moved."

≈

And so on, and so on.
Kids talking, me recording.

And nobody saying we should test them on this
because nobody here is an idiot.

We come to this spot where the falls used to be
to get away.

≈

I know that's ridiculous.
There's no way to get away from Earth.

But two kids have taken up drumming
on a hollow log;

they're even getting good at it.
And three others are sharing the grindstone,

sharpening tools
for our Wall of Rhetorical Questions:

How many words 'til our chisels turn dull?
Answer: The lifespan of butterflies.

How much longer 'til it's better?
What is that, a joke?

≈

We're all still adjusting.
We aren't tundra swans

who've lost their wetlands.
Probably a few of us could migrate

if we could sell our homes,
if anyone would buy them.

Imagine the real estate listing;
that's funny:

"3-bdrm home in a droughtscape,
neighborhood school

distributes gallon-jugs of water,
clawfoot tub."

We're all still adjusting—
there's a girl here who's practicing guitar,

and, mostly, the dogs avoid rattlesnakes,
and we go on.

≈

But it isn't easy.
Say, a kid comes and asks me for a story.

Say, a kid comes and asks for a story
"where my sister gets to eat,

like she's rich or she's a princess or something.
And a boy's in it too—can you do that?...

a boy who's like her brother?
And boys,

even not-by-the-ocean boys,
can learn to swim?"

•

V
Bonds

WHEN WATER WAS STILL AN ELEMENT,

no one needed it in writing.
Lakes were lakes, and you could see them

or wait until spring
after the ice-break.

Rivers would trace the earth's outlines
brown or blue,

like math,
like a set of logical *givens*.

And it *was* a given, and it still is math;
it's the people who are minus signs:

Drain it all faster than it rains or snows,
and there you go.

≈

They elected me to say that,
to be the Listener-Recorder,

to collect their stories,
share them back,

and add my own,
and maybe be a lighthouse too—

part watcher-over, part warning;
it's a growing list.

But we need a different catalog.
Everyone's sick of the wreckage.

They want to remember why it matters
in case it ever rains.

≈

I'm not sure I can do it.
Here's what a guy said this morning.

He said, "The Bering Sea
isn't cold enough now for crabs."

He'd worked those boats,
and there were icebergs.

He'd worked those boats
when he was finished with the Navy.

"The crabs used to number nine billion," he said,
"so zero's less, you know what I'm saying?…

Anyway, I hope you do
'cause I sure don't."

≈

I probably can't do it, not really.
But this is what I know about shoveling,

about missing that work,
and almost the backache too

from the snow's wet weight,
the bending into it.

You stand there, sweating in the cold,
and see results:

see the white banks piling up,
see the sidewalk,

the path to the door,
and you're the one who made that happen,

you and cold,
you and quiet

since the traffic's down
and the tire-sounds are muffled.

Then you carve out a place for your wife to park.
And then she's home.

≈

And there were daffodils too,
these yellow cups rising through the dirt.

They'd shoulder their way past winter,
then fill up with rain.

≈

She says, "They always had almonds
in the grocery store.

How is that even possible?"

≈

He says, "I wish I would've
stood in that waterfall

when it was here."

≈

One friend remembers her sister.
She says, "At least she died

before the worst of it.
Seeing this river empty

would've made her cry.
She used to come rafting here."

One friend used to be a ski instructor.
And one kid brings me a map.

He's fourteen,
above-average angry:

"You mean, this was real?
Like all of this blue was really water?"

One friend always wears
steel-toed boots,

and his daughter's always wearing
that butterfly costume.

"I have to," she says, "so they can find me.
And I'll bring one to you."

•

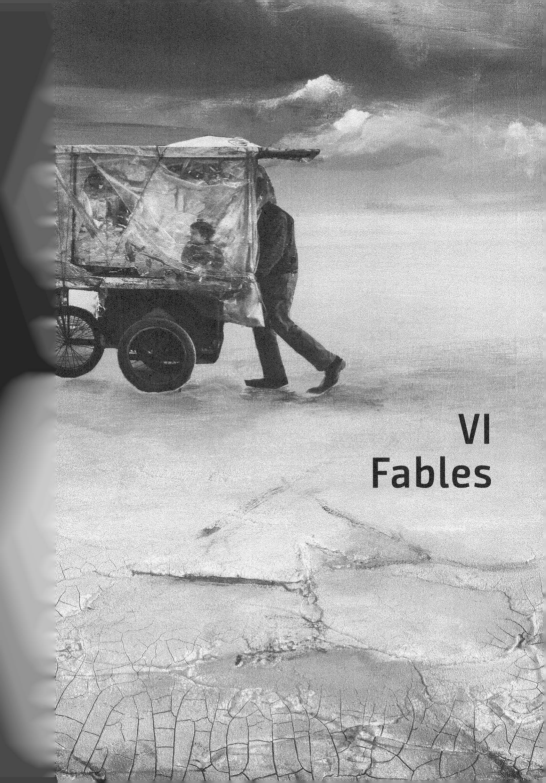

**VI
Fables**

NEW TIMES CALL FOR NEW FABLES,

so twice a year we listen,
make March and September our story months

and arrive: alone, or in pairs,
or in families.

We sit on the rocks
where the falls used to be

and begin,
or we gather on the sandbar.

We set down lanterns at our feet,
or build a low fire.

This isn't a ritual;
the only point of it is stories.

Sometimes the moon is full,
and others not.

≈

The bear had a cave,
a good one,

with vines hanging wild
above the mouth of it,

and only two miles to a lake
with shoreline pools

where the fish
just waited to be eaten,

where mushrooms, none of them poison,
plumped from dirt.

But the bear looked around,
and the bear wanted more.

He had claws, so he dug himself a hollow.
Then a channel to his own front door.

And then the water flowed right to him,
bringing fish, even offering

his own reflection,
which was good;

≈

at least it seemed to be
until the other bears did it too—

taking the lake
like it belonged to them

and not deer, not moose,
not to crows and the gravel in their voices—

they took from the lake
until only the bed of it was left.

Now all of their caves
are just as empty.

≈

The birds tried singing to the sky
to bring them rain,

but nothing happened.
They tied melodies to the wind's tail

so their songs could reach up higher,
but nothing changed—

the rains didn't come,
and the days weren't green.

No leaves
to hide their nests behind.

No flowering shrubs with their seedheads.
And no snow in the winter either,

so how could there be spring
with all of the streambeds empty?

The birds didn't wait for an answer.
They already knew.

≈

Might as well reason with a rattlesnake
as hear more talk about progress

because that word comes with a hiss;
it's built right in.

They'll tell you that their word means *more*.
And then they'll bite.

≈

The heron looked down and saw rivers
wider than its wings,

but it also saw people.
They'll need stillness, it thought,

and tried to teach them,
but the people didn't see.

≈

The sky is the father of lightning;
and lightning is the mother of storms;

and storms are the mother of rivers,
every fork, each flash

and cascade over cliff-edge;
and cliffs

are the sisters of gravity;
and gravity's the brother of facts;

and facts are the parents of everything, even us,
unlikely as it seems sometimes;

and we are the parents of tomorrow;
and tomorrow is the mother of hope;

and hope is the sister of lightning,
thunder, rain…

≈

Most times, nobody speaks now.
We let our lanterns

fold back the night.
Or the low fire settles into coals

that take their time,
as if they're still thinking.

Sleep would be fine,
but there isn't any hurry

since an owl might wake
and add its echo.

Or a cloud might glide across the moon
and be something to see.

•

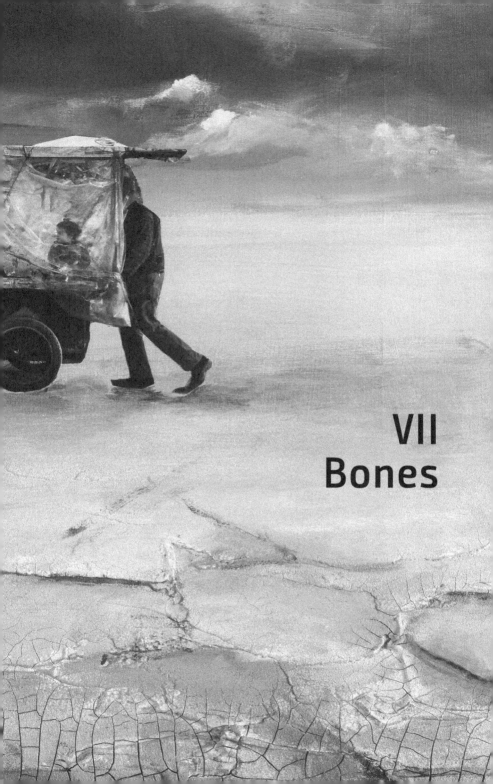

VII
Bones

THE BONES, OF COURSE,

make interesting litter.
Cattle, mostly,

but sometimes coyotes too.
Go eight days without water, you're a camel.

Do that as anything else,
and you're a ghost,

a voice leaving on the wind
and rising away.

≈

The stars shine brighter now
with midnight blackouts mandatory.

They switch off the grid to save water,
what little there is,

and too late
for this bighorn sheep,

for these ravens—
a bleached white pair.

≈

A kid wrote this letter to the future:

Dear Future,

    If I could, I would hand you this letter myself, but I don't know where you'll be when I get there. My mom says it wasn't always like this, with everything drought. That means no more water.

    We still have bathtubs and sinks, but nothing comes out. The faucets are empty. And we still have glasses in the cupboard but mostly use canteens, and you only take sips is all.

    If you already know that, I hope not, not unless it's in a book. I like to read books, even sad ones, but maybe you're ok, and you don't have asthma, and don't have to hide on the dustcloud days.

    And maybe there's a swimming pool that's full so you can jump in.

≈

And another wrote this letter to the past:

Dear Before, when I wasn't even born yet,

How come you used up everything? I guess you weren't trying

to be mean, but it isn't fair. I wish I could make a snowman instead

of just be cold.

We have a dog now because the man died who took care of her.

She doesn't even cry when she's thirsty, she's a good dog.

When I point to the sky and say the clouds used to live there, she

looks up too and wags her tail.

≈

And a woman just handed me a postcard with this on the back:

Snow on Timpanogos.

So you know how it looked

when I was growing up.
                    LOVE, DAD

≈

And a girl sent this one to the governor:

Dear Sir,

Were you actually serious when you told us we need to pray for rain? That isn't a plan of action, or governing at all. I do not pray that I will graduate. I do the work, absurd as it is sometimes.

Take, for example, three classes in Science when adults like you ignore scientists. Or take Civics, for example: I am still too young to vote.

But I won't be next year.

Sincerely,

≈

They asked me to record these things,
to be the Listener and Reservoir and Scribe—

as if our letters,
and losses,

and stories
are scattered bones,

and maybe
I can fit them together.

So we still remember
in these drought times.

So we still imagine
in these drought times.

And so one day, if anyone finds this record,
we'll seem whole,

≈

like we were people.

•

VIII
Rain

IF THE DROUGHT BREAKS,

some of us will stand amazed
just listening to downspouts,

to the rain—old song we'd forgotten—
running through,

and out,
and over the hard-parched ground.

What's that? That's mud,
a discovery.

And what's that? That thing
is called a snail.

If it's here,
it means something will be growing soon.

Irises, maybe.
Like the color in the center of our eyes.

≈

"If the drought breaks,
I want to know what skinny-dipping feels like."

"If the drought breaks,
I want to smell the rain."

"If the drought breaks,
I want to wash the windows,

wash them clean,
all that caked-on dust—

a whole decade—
disappeared...

can you imagine it?
You're sitting by the living room window,

and it's clear now, and you can look out
at whatever's going by."

≈

And so on, and so on;
people talking, me recording.

It's our way of filling up the margins
like a cup

that we don't have to ration.
It's our way

of keeping the clock-hands
from coming to a stop.

≈

That's what a drought does—
stop.

All the clouds you looked at, or didn't—
stop.

All the rain—stop,
turning things green—stop,

just a word
they printed in the dictionary.

All the snowfall—stop,
spring melting—stop,

so the rivers
we need to keep living—stop.

And the lakes. The water from our faucets.
Everything stops.

≈

But not when we gather here
in this spot where the falls used to be,

hiking like amateur pilgrims,
alone or in pairs.

There's a flat slab
perfect for our discard relics,

all the bits
this droughtscape doesn't need:

fishing poles,
an ice-cube tray,

a lapel pin "For 25 Years of Service,"
and a stack

of certified envelopes
stamped, "Collection Due."

Any idiot can send those threats.
It takes more work to remember,

and find others still trying to remember too,
and say hello.

≈

And if the drought breaks,
maybe in the months ahead

someone will open up a nursery.
And someone will plant a rose bush—

just for red.
For that smell when the wind leans in.

≈

And if it breaks,
then maybe in the years to come

the forests floors
will open.

Through all the downed trees,
over blackened slopes—

now deer.
And the aspen returning.

≈

Which reminds me of a story:

For the wedding of the forest and the moon,
everyone was there,

even wolves
stepping out from the treeline;

even wolves who'd be gone soon,
loping into memory…

The moon and the forest were beautiful,
and everyone arrived—

the river and falls
to add music,

and the rain coming down
to be a witness,

and the sky gave the Future as a gift.
But it didn't say what kind.

•

Acknowledgments

Thank you to the editors of the following in which these first appeared:

"Section II: Gathering" (under the title "Back When Water Was an Element") was a finalist for the 2022 C.P. Cavafy Prize and appeared in *Poetry International Online* (Fall 2023).

"Section III: Reconstructing Fragments" (under the title "from The Book of Drought") appeared in *Terrain.org* (10 Jan. 2024).

"Section IV: Lessons" (under the title "Kids Cut Right Through the Nonsense") won the Milton Kessler Memorial Prize in Poetry from *Harpur Palate Magazine* and appeared in issue 22.1 (Summer 2023).

"Section V: Bonds" (under the title "When Water Was Still an Element") won the *Peatsmoke* Summer Poetry Contest and appeared in *Peatsmoke Journal* (Fall 2023).

"Section VII: Bones" (under the title "The Bones, of Course") won First Place in the *Letter Review* Prize for Poetry (29 May 2023).

Sections I, II, V, and VII (under the title "Drought & Bones") won First Place in the 2023 Utah Original Writing Competition from the Utah Division of Arts & Museums.

About the Author

PHOTO BY JENNIFER WOZNICK

ROB CARNEY is the author of eight previous books of poems, most recently *Call and Response* (Black Lawrence Press 2021) and *The Book of Sharks* (Black Lawrence 2018), which won the 15 Bytes Book Award. He is a recipient of the Milton Kessler Memorial Prize in Poetry, the Robinson Jeffers/Tor House Foundation Award for Poetry, and he has written a featured series called "Old Roads, New Stories" for the award-winning online journal *Terrain.org* for the last nine years. Carney has read his work on national public radio and at conferences, festivals, and universities across the country. Favorite drink: coffee. Favorite animal: the Great White. He is a Professor of English at Utah Valley University and lives in Salt Lake City.